A Hands-On, Minds-On Approach

Grades 4-5

Written by
Beth Davis

Cover Design by
Matthew Van Zomeren

Inside Art by
Elizabeth Adams

Published by Instructional Fair • TS Denison
an imprint of

About the Book

The Inquiry Science series was designed and tested by classroom teachers familiar with the National Science Education standards. It is the goal of the series to apply the standards in a user-friendly format.

Promote minds-on learning by challenging students to verbalize their observations and make inferences. Ask simple questions such as the following: "What just happened? Why do you think that happened? What did you discover? Where have you seen that before?" You may raise students' awareness and highlight the importance of the science process skills through discussion.

Credits

Author: Beth Davis
Cover Design: Matthew Van Zomeren
Inside Illustrations: Elizabeth Adams
Project Director/Editor: Elizabeth Flikkema
Editors: Wendy Roh Jenks,
  Meredith Van Zomeren
Page Design: Pat Geasler

About The Author

Beth Davis is an outstanding educator from Miami, Florida, where she is currently a science lab teacher for grades 2-5. Ms. Davis received her bachelor of science in elementary education from Florida International University. Her master's degree was earned at Nova University. Beth Davis has written curriculum and several articles in the areas of math and science. Her other McGraw-Hill Children's Publishing books include *Flowering Plants* and *Matter*.

McGraw-Hill
Children's Publishing
A Division of The McGraw·Hill Companies

Published by Instructional Fair • TS Denison
An imprint of McGraw-Hill Children's Publishing
Copyright © 2000 McGraw-Hill Children's Publishing

Limited Reproduction Permission: Permission to duplicate these materials is limited to the person for whom they are purchased. Reproduction for an entire school or school district is unlawful and strictly prohibited.

Send all inquiries to:
McGraw-Hill Children's Publishing
3195 Wilson Drive NW
Grand Rapids, Michigan 49544

All Rights Reserved • Printed in the United States of America

Electricity & Magnetism—grades 4–5
ISBN: 1-56822-950-X

3 4 5 6 7 8 9 PHXBK 07 06 05 04 03

Table of Contents

Magnetic Attraction
Exploring attraction & repulsion . .4–5

Making a Compass
Learning how a compass actually works .6–7

Mapping a Magnet
Finding the north and south pole of a magnet 8–9

Magnetizing Metals
Magnetizing metal objects 10–11

Magnetic Fields
Exploring magnetic fields 12–13

Are All Metals Magnetic?
Discovering what metals are not magnetic 14–15

Is There Really Iron in Cereals?
Testing breakfast cereals for iron 16–17

Exploring Electromagnets
Using a battery to create an electromagnet 18–19

Recycled Battery Holder
Creating a homemade bulb holder. 20–21

Flashing the Light
Lighting a flashlight bulb. 22–23

Conductors and Insulators
Tracing the flow of electricity . . .24–25

Make Your Own Light Bulb
Constructing homemade light bulbs 26–27

Static Electricity and Bubbles
Conducting static electricity 28–29

Make Your Own Lightning
Simulating lightning with a pan, fork, and plastic sheet. 30–31

Performance-Based Assessment
A rubric of student performance . . .32

© Instructional Fair • TS Denison

IF20857 *Electricity & Magnetism*

Magnetic Attraction

Gearing Up

Open a can in front of the class with an electric can opener. Lead the students to wonder why the can stayed suspended while the can opener worked. A magnet holds the can in place. You may wish to carefully allow each child a chance to attach a can to the can opener. Brainstorm other familiar things that might contain a magnet.

Process Skills Used
- predicting
- recording data
- observing
- classifying
- graphing

Guided Discovery

Background for the teacher:

A magnet is an object that attracts (brings near) metals such as iron and steel. The ends of a magnet are called poles. A magnet has a north pole and a south pole. Opposite poles attract; the north pole of one magnet attracts the south pole of another magnet. Like poles repel; the north pole of one magnet pushes away the north pole of another magnet.

Materials needed for each group:

magnets

objects to explore: wood block, thread, steel pin, aluminum foil, copper wire, paper clip, penny, shoelace, plastic straw, steel wool, nail, metal can, metal spoon

Directions for the activity:

Have students fill in the prediction column of the data table to indicate whether items will be attracted to magnets. Then, allow them time to explore and find out which items are attracted to magnets. Have the students sort the objects into two groups: items that are attracted to magnets, and those that are not.

Responding to Discovery

Lead students to make conclusions as to what items are attracted to magnets. Help students to realize that all metals are not magnetic.

Applications and Extensions

Think about how magnets are used to make our lives easier. Write about some magnets we use in everyday life.

Real-World Applications
- Discuss how inventors use magnets.
- Discuss when you wouldn't want a metal to be magnetic.

© Instructional Fair • TS Denison   IF20857 *Electricity & Magnetism*

Name _____

Magnetic Attraction

🌿 First, make a prediction, then test each item. Hold each item next to the magnet to determine whether it is magnetic. Write your observations below on the chart.

Item	Your prediction	Is it magnetic?	What is it made of?
wood block			
thread			
steel pin			
aluminum foil			
copper wire			
paper clip			
penny			
shoelace			
steel wool			
nail			
metal can			
metal spoon			
plastic straw			

🌿 Were there any items that surprised you? _____

🌿 What did you observe about the magnetic items? _____

🌿 Sort the items into two groups. Draw a picture of each item in its proper category.

magnetic	non-magnetic

© Instructional Fair • TS Denison   IF20857 Electricity & Magnetism

Making a Compass

Gearing Up

You probably have the walls in your classroom labeled north, south, west, and east. Ask the students to explain how they know the north wall is north other than "My teacher says it is." Lead them to ask for proof. You can provide proof with a compass. Obtain several different styles of compasses to show that they all point to north.

> *Process Skills Used*
> - following directions
> - observing
> - recording data

Guided Discovery

Background for the teacher:

The compass has been used for a long time to help navigators find directions. A magnetic compass is an instrument that indicates direction. The compass needle always points to the magnetic North Pole. When you have established north, you can determine the other directions by their relationship to north. In this lesson, students will make their own compass.

Materials needed for each group:

a magnet   straight pin

small square of Styrofoam (from a meat tray)

plastic bowl   water

loose staples in a dish (one for the whole class)

Directions for the activity:

Demonstrate to students that the pin is not a magnet by holding the pin in a container of loose staples. Then have each group rub the head of a pin back and forth 40 times on one side of the magnet. Then have them put their magnetized pins in the dish of staples again to show that it is now a magnet. Once the pin is magnetized, students poke it through the Styrofoam square so that the pin is sticking out on both sides. Float the Styrofoam with the pin in a horizontal position in a bowl of water. The water should be just deep enough so that the pin and Styrofoam move freely. Be sure that all magnets are put away as they will interfere with the compass. Instruct the students to turn the pin in either direction. They will find that it will turn back to the original direction. The pin is pointing to north and south poles.

Responding to Discovery

Ask students what might happen if a magnet were placed near the pin once it was in the water.

Applications and Extensions

How might a compass be useful for finding constellations?

> *Real-World Applications*
> - Discuss how hikers use a compass and a map.
> - Discuss how pilots use a compass to navigate.

Name _____

Making a Compass

- Draw what happened when your teacher held a pin in a pile of loose staples.

- Magnetize the pin by rubbing it back and forth 40 times on one side of a magnet. Draw what happened when you held the magnetized pin in a pile of loose staples.

- Poke the magnetized pin sideways through the styrofoam and place it in a small amount of water. Draw the pin in the water and label the directions (north, south, west, and east).

- Turn the floating pin a half turn and let it go. Explain what happened.

_____

- How is what you created like a compass? _____

_____

© Instructional Fair • TS Denison   IF20857 *Electricity & Magnetism*

Mapping a Magnet

Gearing Up

Obtain several different maps. Include road maps, classroom and school maps, state and world maps. Discuss ways that maps can be helpful.

Process Skills Used
- communicating
- comparing
- recording data
- experimenting

Guided Discovery

Background for the teacher:

Just as the earth has a north and a south pole, a magnet also has a north and south pole. If a magnet is broken in half, it will still have a north and a south pole. You can use a compass to map, or label, the poles of a magnet.

Materials needed for each group:

two magnets

one compass

12 cm of masking tape

pen or pencil

Directions for the activity:

Demonstrate how to map the poles of a magnet. Place 1 inch of masking tape on each end or side of the two magnets. Hold one end/side of the magnet to the side of the compass. Observe the compass needle. Write N or S on the masking tape to indicate the compass direction (north or south). Flip the magnet and hold the magnet to the compass again. Label the other side of the magnet. Have the students repeat these steps to map, or label, their two magnets. Allow groups time to explore how the north and south poles react to each other and different magnetic surfaces.

Responding to Discovery

Discuss how the north and south poles react to each other and different magnetic surfaces.

Applications and Extensions

Do magnets work under water? Through clothing? Test the attraction of opposite poles of the magnets through different substances.

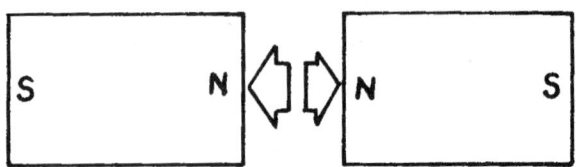

Real-World Applications
- Research life on the North and South Poles.
- What does the saying "opposites attract" mean?

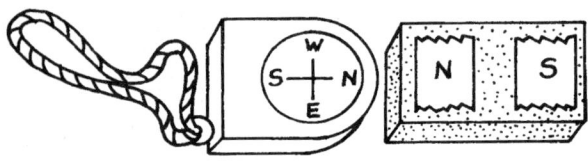

Name _____

Mapping a Magnet

1. Place 2-3 cm of masking tape on each end or side of the two magnets.

2. Hold one end/side of the magnet to the side of the compass.

3. Observe the compass needle. Write N or S on the masking tape to indicate the compass direction (north or south).

4. Flip the magnet and hold the magnet to the compass again. Label the other side of the magnet.

5. Repeat these steps to "map" or label the second magnet.

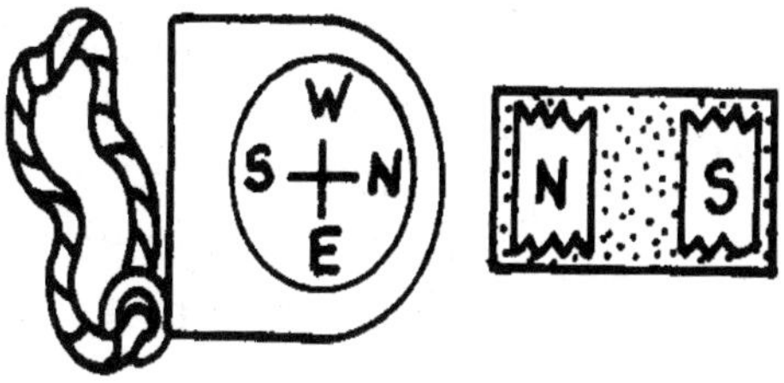

 Explore how the north and south poles react to each other and different magnetic surfaces.

1. Hold the "N" of one magnet to the "N" of the other magnet.

    Did the magnets attract or repel? _____

2. Hold the "S" of one magnet to the "S" of the other magnet.

    Did the magnets attract or repel? _____

3. Predict what will happen when the "S" of one magnet is placed next to the "N" of the other magnet. _____

4. Test your prediction and explain what happened. _____
    _____

5. Draw a picture of two magnets that are attracted to each other.

6. Draw a picture of two magnets that repel each other here.

© Instructional Fair • TS Denison   IF20857 Electricity & Magnetism

Magnetizing Metals

Gearing Up

Hold up two forks and ask the class to tell you what they are. They should say "forks." Tell them that they are mistaken; it is a flashlight. Arrange the forks so they touch the bottom and top of a battery and light a bulb. Let's explore today how we can make another everyday object perform a new task.

Process Skills Used
- observing
- recording data
- predicting
- forming a hypothesis

Guided Discovery

Background for the teacher:

Some metals can be magnetized so that they function as a magnet. A steel straight pin is magnetized by rubbing it on a magnet in one direction. The more stokes against the magnet, the greater the magnetic strength.

Material needed for each group:

a steel pin for each student

a bar magnet (more than one per group is nice)

small paperclips

Safety tip: warn students to be careful with the sharp end of the pin.

Directions for the activity:

Before beginning, instruct students to hold their pins in a pile of paper clips to show that the pins are not magnetic. Each student strokes the side of a pin across the top of the magnet about 50 times in one direction (not back and forth). Then, students place the pin inside the pile of paper clips again and count how many clips are picked up.

Responding to Discovery

Ask students to describe what happened. Discuss how a magnet can pass it's magnetism to another object. Discuss why students think they must stroke in one direction only. Discuss why they must stroke so many times. Discuss what other objects they could magnetize.

Applications and Extensions

Have students explore other objects in the classroom to determine what objects can be magnetized.

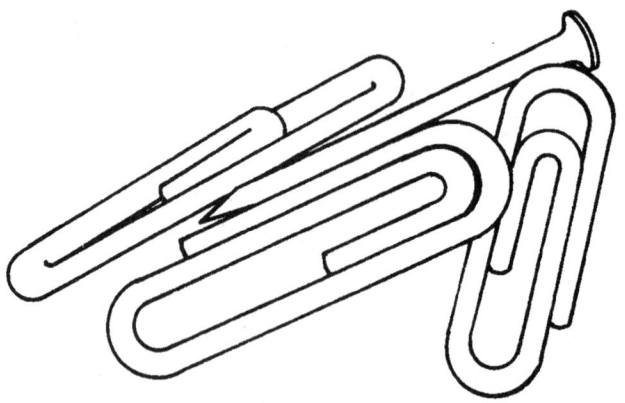

Real-World Applications

Discuss how high-speed trains in Japan and Germany use magnets to operate. The trains are magnetically propelled across the tracks at a very high speed of up to 500 km per hour.

© Instructional Fair • TS Denison IF20857 *Electricity & Magnetism*

Magnetizing Metals

Name _____

• Stroke the pin across the magnet 50 times in one direction. Hold the magnetized pin in the paper clips. Count how many paperclips the pin picked up.
_____

• What do you think will happen if you stroke the magnet more than 50 times?
_____

• Stroke a pin 75 times across a magnet. How many clips did you get this time?
_____

• Do you think you can magnetize other materials? Make a list of materials you would like to try. Predict what will happen and try to magnetize the items. Record your observations.

Item	Prediction	How many clips did it pick up?
_____	_____	_____
_____	_____	_____
_____	_____	_____
_____	_____	_____

• Do you think it makes a difference if you stroke the pin toward the north or south pole of the magnet? _____

What steps do you need to go through to test your hypothesis? _____
_____
_____

Try your hypothesis.

© Instructional Fair • TS Denison   IF20857 Electricity & Magnetism

Magnetic Fields

Gearing Up

Very strong magnets are used to lift cars and other metals in scrap metal shops. A strong magnetic field allows the magnet to pick up the car. Hold your hand flat and pour some iron filings in the palm of your hand. Pass a magnet under your hand. Did the magnetic field go through your hand to move the filings?

Process Skills Used
- recording data
- observing
- predicting
- classifying
- communicating

Guided Discovery

Background for the teacher:

The earth is surrounded by a magnetic field. Imagine there is a large bar magnet buried inside the earth. The poles of this imaginary magnet are located near the North and South poles. Scientists think that the Earth's magnetism may be produced from the huge iron core and the rapid spinning of the earth.

Material needed for each group:

iron filings

plastic baggie to hold the magnet

bar magnet

materials: glass jar, aluminum pan, thin block of wood, paper, water in a sealed plastic bag

Directions for the activity:

Students will test whether the bar magnet can move the iron filings through the different materials listed on the chart on page 13.

Teacher tip: Have students put their magnet in the baggie. If the iron filings touch the magnet, simply remove the magnet from the bag and the filings will fall off. Otherwise, it is very difficult to remove the filings from the magnet.

Responding to Discovery

Have students calculate the percentage of their correct predictions. Discuss what the results say about the ability of magnetic fields to pass through different materials. Discuss what students actually observed that told them the magnetic field passed through the material.

Applications and Extensions

Change the thickness of the materials in the experiment to determine whether that makes a difference in the magnetic field passing through it.

Real-World Applications

Magnets are now being used to clean fish tanks. One magnet is placed on the outside of the glass and one is placed on the inside. The magnet penetrates the glass and moves back and forth to clean the tank.

© Instructional Fair • TS Denison IF20857 Electricity & Magnetism

Name _____
Magnetic Fields

❧ Before you test each item, make your predictions on the chart. Place the filings on one side of the material. Place the magnet on the other side. Observe whether the magnetic field passes through the material.

Item	Your prediction	Item's response
paper	_____	_____
wood	_____	_____
glass	_____	_____
aluminum	_____	_____
plastic	_____	_____
water in a sealed bag	_____	_____

❧ Draw a picture for each item to show how the filings responded.

Are All Metals Magnetic?

Gearing Up

Have you ever wondered if all metals are equally magnetic? Try this simple test to see. Try to pick up a quarter with a magnet. Now try a steel pin. Was there a difference?

Process Skills Used
- predicting
- calculating
- recording data
- graphing
- experimenting
- following directions

Guided Discovery

Background for the teacher:

Most materials, even wood, copper, and water do not seem to respond to magnets. Actually, all materials can respond to magnetic force, but some so weakly that the force is not observable in everyday life. Items that respond well to magnets are iron, nickel, and cobalt.

Materials for each group:

magnet

sharpened pencil (graphite)

straight pin (steel)

aluminum foil

copper wire

paper clip (steel)

penny (copper-plated zinc)

steel wool

nail (iron)

aluminum can

dime (copper and nickel)

Directions for the activity:

Students test each of the items for its reaction to the magnet. Have students complete the table. They should research the composition of the different metal items (content is in parentheses in the materials list).

Responding to Discovery

Study and discuss the completed table. Have students determine what types of metals are always magnetic. What types of metals are not attracted to the magnet?

Applications and Extensions

Have students collect as many different metals as they can find. From what they know about different types of metals, have them predict which ones will be attracted to a magnet and which ones will not.

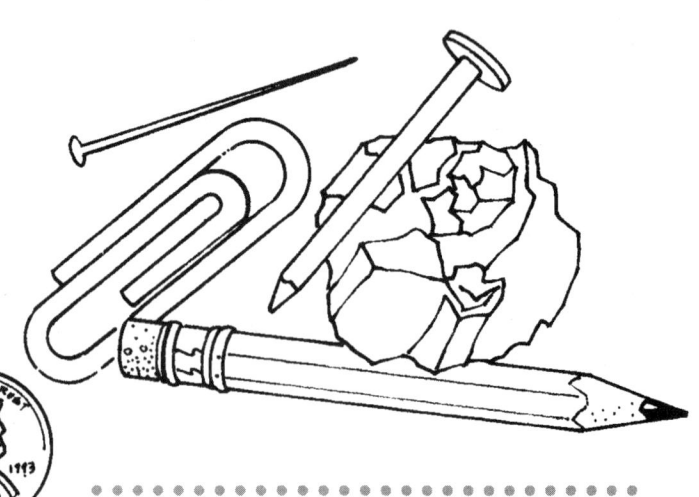

Real-World Applications
Discuss how mechanics may magnetize their screwdrivers to retrieve lost screws.

© Instructional Fair • TS Denison

IF20857 *Electricity & Magnetism*

Name _____

Are All Metals Magnetic?

🍂 List the items being tested in the table. Predict and then test each item against a magnet. Record whether each item is magnetic or nonmagnetic.

Item	Your prediction	Is it magnetic?	What is it made of?

🍂 Research the items to determine their composition. Study the table.

What types of metals are always magnetic?

_____

What types of metals are never magnetic?

_____

Is There Really Iron in Cereals?

Gearing Up

Discuss with students that their parents probably want them to eat cereal that contains vitamins and minerals because vitamins and minerals are healthy. Reproduce the nutritional information on two boxes of iron-fortified cereal, such as Total and Quaker oatmeal. Have students find out how much of each mineral is in the cereals and what percentage that is of the recommended daily allowance.

Process Skills Used
- reading a table
- observing
- recording data

Guided Discovery

Background for the teacher:

In this experiment, students are separating a mixture. Students have learned that iron is a magnetic material. This will help them come up with a plan for removing iron from the cereal. In separating minerals from rocks, other methods include acidic or caustic water, gravity separation, or flotation. For example, gravity separation is used in gold panning. Students will be surprised to find that their cereal contains iron filings.

Materials for each pair or group:

1 cup (237 ml) iron-fortified cold cereal (Total)

2 cups (474 ml) hot water

one clear drinking glass

a bar magnet wrapped in plastic wrap secured with a twistie

Directions for the activity:

Select a sample of cereal that is iron-fortified, such as Total. Students add hot water to make a slurry and stir with the magnet until the cereal is soggy. The longer the cereal is stirred, the more complete the iron removal. 30 minutes gives the maximum iron recovery. Students remove the magnet and remove the plastic wrap over a sheet of white paper. The particles of iron will fall to the paper. Hold the magnet below the paper to show that they are attracted to the magnet.

Responding to Discovery

Compare student findings. Compare how long students kept the magnets in the mixture to the amount of iron that was separated. Ask students how they think they could measure the amount of iron separated from the cereal.

Applications and Extensions

What other fortified food product could be used instead of cold cereal? What other methods could they use to separate the mixture?

Real-World Applications
- Discuss the importance of iron in the diet
- Research how scientists find creative ways to separate mixtures

© Instructional Fair • TS Denison

IF20857 *Electricity & Magnetism*

Name _____

Is There Really Iron in Cereals?

- Look at the nutritional information on two different cereal boxes. Fill in the table to show how much of each mineral is present in each.

Mineral name	Cereal one	Cereal two
_____	_____	_____
_____	_____	_____
_____	_____	_____
_____	_____	_____
_____	_____	_____

- Do you think you can measure the actual amount of iron in the cereal? To do this, you will need to separate the mixture that makes up the cereal. Follow the directions to separate the iron from the rest of the cereal.

    1. Pour a cup of iron-fortified cereal in a glass.
    2. Add hot water to make a slurry and stir with the magnet.
    3. Keep track of how long you stir. Observe the dark slivers of iron attached to the magnetic bar. Remove the plastic wrap over a sheet of white paper.

    How long did you stir the cereal? _____

    Describe what you saw once the magnet was removed from the cereal. What do you think the black pieces are. How do you know? _____
    _____

- Repeat the experiment with the other cereal.

    How long did you stir the cereal? _____

    Describe what you saw once the magnet was removed from the cereal. _____
    _____

© Instructional Fair • TS Denison   IF20857 *Electricity & Magnetism*

Exploring Electromagnets

Gearing Up

Touch a steel or iron nail to a pile of small paper clips. Did the nail pick up the paper clips? Discuss why it didn't. Ask the students if there might be a way to magnetize the nail. Try their suggestions. Then, tell them that today they will be making this nail into an electromagnet.

Process Skills Used

- observing
- recording data
- predicting
- making a model
- comparing

Guided Discovery

Background for the teacher:

Magnetism is produced by the motion of electrical charges. You can magnetize a conductor of electricity, such as a nail, by running current through the conductor. The more coils of wire that are wrapped around the nail, the stronger the electromagnet will become. The smaller the battery, the less magnetism will be produced.

Material needed per group:

one 6-volt lantern battery

large iron or steel nail

30 small paperclips

insulated wire cut in the following lengths: 35 cm, 50 cm, and 65 cm (Strip the insulation from both ends of the wires.)

Directions for the activity:

Show the students how to wrap a wire around the nail leaving 5 cm of wire unwrapped at each end. In each group, the students should tightly wrap the 35 cm wire around the nail.

Then, the students attach the wire ends to the different ends of the battery. (Be careful, some heat is given off.)

Students hold the pointed end of the nail in the pile of clips and lift. They record the number of paper clips picked up.

Students repeat the same process with each length of wire.

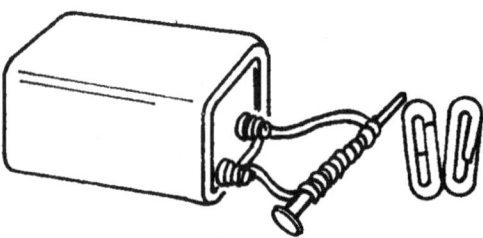

Responding to Discovery

Discuss what happened to the nail when the electric current ran around it.

Applications and Extensions

Discuss how students could change variables to increase or reduce the strength of the electromagnet (tighter or looser coils, larger or smaller nail, larger or smaller battery).

Real-World Applications

- Discuss how electromagnets are used in car starters, doorbells, can openers, and telephones.

Name _____
Exploring Electromagnets

🍃 Before the wire was attached to the battery, did the nail pick up any paper clips? Explain why or why not. _____

_____

Draw the nail wrapped in the wire attached to the battery.	Draw your electromagnet approaching a pile of paperclips.

🍃 Record how many paper clips your electromagnet picked up.

Lenth of wire	Number of clips picked up
35 cm	_____
50 cm	_____
60 cm	_____

How many paper clips do you think a 80 cm wire electromagnet will pick up?

_____

🍃 What else could you change to affect the number of paper clips your electromagnet picks up? _____

_____

🍃 What could you use besides a nail to make an electromagnet? _____

_____

Recycled Battery Holder

Gearing Up:

Discuss the reasons why people recycle. The three Rs of recycling are reduce, reuse, and recycle. In today's activity, the students will reuse an empty toilet paper roll to make a recycled battery holder.

Process Skills Used
- following a sequence
- measuring
- communicating
- making a model

Guided Discovery

Background for the teacher:

Rather than purchase a specialized battery holder for exploring electricity concepts, practice recycling by making this battery holder from an empty toilet paper roll.

Material needed for each holder:

D-cell battery

toilet paper tube

two 3 inch (7.5 cm) nails

two thick rubber bands

two sheets of aluminum foil

two 30 cm pieces of wire with stripped ends

two washers

strips of newspaper (width of battery)

Directions for the activity:

Students follow the directions on page 21 to make a recycled battery holder. In advance, you will need to strip the ends off the insulated wire with a knife. Guide students carefully through this experiment. Warn them to be careful with any sharp objects, such as the nails. There is potential for injury when they poke the nails through the tube. You may wish to have them work over a soft surface, such as Styrofoam to absorb the pressure.

Responding to Discovery

Ask students to trace how the energy from the battery moves through the conductors in this homemade battery holder. Have students propose explanations for why it is important to strip the ends of the insulated wire?

Applications and Extensions

Use the battery holder to light a bulb and demonstrate parallel and series circuits.

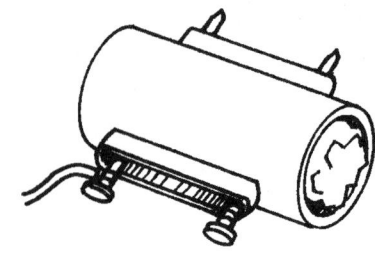

Real-World Applications
Compare how the body of a flashlight is like a battery holder.

© Instructional Fair • TS Denison   IF20857 *Electricity & Magnetism*

Name _____

Recycled Battery Holder

1. Wrap newspaper strips around the battery so it will fit snugly in the tube. Be certain that the paper does not go past the ends of the battery.

2. Slide the wrapped battery into the center of the toilet paper tube. Mark the tube to indicate the positive and negative ends of the battery.

3. Gently crumple the aluminum foil. Place a foil ball in each end of the tube so they touch the ends of the battery.

4. Carefully push the nails through the walls of the tube and through the foil.

5. Put a rubber band over the two nails on each side. The rubber bands should be tight enough to put pressure on the nails.

6. Wrap one stripped end of each wire to the heads of the nails. Attach a washer to each of the loose ends.

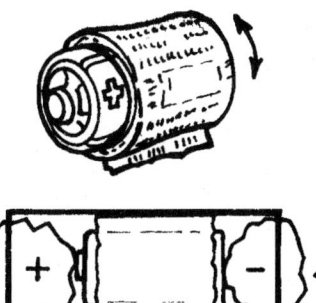

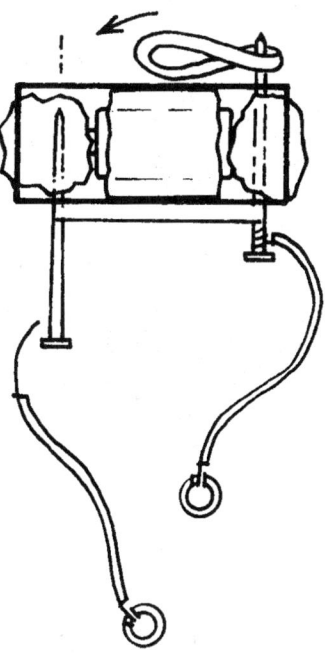

🍂 Does the foil serve as a conductor or an insulator? _____

🍂 What is the source of energy in this setup? _____

🍂 Explain how the current passes from the battery to the washers.

_____

🍂 Draw a picture of how you could use two battery holders together to light a bulb.

© Instructional Fair • TS Denison   IF20857 *Electricity & Magnetism*

Flashing the Light

Gearing Up

Shine a flashlight around the room. Ask the students if they have ever taken apart a flashlight to see how it works. Talk about the setup of the flashlight as you take it apart. Note the arrangement of the batteries and the connection to the bulb. Point out how the switch connects and disconnects the circuit.

Process Skills Used
- making a model
- predicting
- forming a hypothesis
- communicating

Guided Discovery

Background for the teacher:

A battery, otherwise known as a dry cell, is a source of energy. The larger the battery, the more energy that can be stored and used. By using multiple batteries, students can cause the light to burn brighter. Large electrical items, such as a radio, use more batteries than a flashlight. A D-cell battery is not strong enough to harm the students, although they might feel some heat given off. Inform students that they should not experiment with electrical outlets at home. They can get hurt using that type of electricity.

Material needed for each group:

one D-cell battery holder (see Recycled Battery Holder activity)

flashlight bulb

Directions for the activity:

Explain to students that the flow of electricity follows a circular path. When you turn on a light, you complete a circuit so an electric current can flow to a light bulb. Challenge the students to figure out how to light the bulb and form a complete circuit. Teacher tip: In order for the bulb to light, one washer must be on the contact point and the other washer should be on the metal casing that holds the bulb. **Note:** *if the attached washers repeatedly come in contact with each other, it could damage the battery.*

Responding to Discovery

Students draw pictures of the different arrangements they tried to light the bulb. Have them write a description of the arrangement that worked. Discuss the flow of energy in the circuit.

Applications and Extensions

Make a battery holder for three batteries using a paper towel roll.

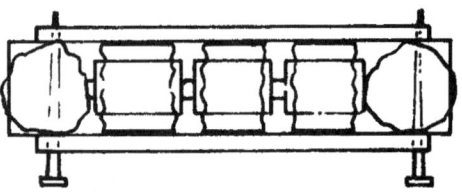

Real-World Applications
Demonstrate how different sized batteries are used for different size flashlights.

Flashing the Light

Name _____

- Draw a plan for how you will connect the bulb to your battery holder and light the bulb. Label all the parts.

- Explain how your drawing shows a complete circuit. Build your model.
  _____
  _____

- Try other arrangements until you make the bulb light. Draw the arrangement that works below. Label all the parts.

- Explain how your model completes the circuit. _____
  _____

- Bonus: Try another configuration using two battery holders.

© Instructional Fair • TS Denison 23 IF20857 *Electricity & Magnetism*

Conductors and Insulators

Gearing Up

Ask the students to reflect on what they know about the flow of electricity in a circuit. Can they think of anything that would stop, or interrupt, the flow of electricity? Use a piece of tape to attach a wire to the bottom of a D-cell battery. Attach the other end to the side of a light bulb. Put your finger on top of the battery between the bulb and the battery. Ask the students to describe what happened and explain why.

Process Skills Used
- predicting
- observing
- drawing conclusions
- recording data

Guided Discovery

Background for the teacher:

An item that stops electrons from flowing freely is called an insulator. An item that allows electric current to flow freely is called a conductor.

Materials needed per group:

one D-cell battery

20 cm of insulated wire with the ends stripped

one flashlight bulb

tape

potential conductors and insulators: eraser, Popsicle stick, sponge, pencil, paper, cardboard, plastic lid, penny, aluminum foil, metal key, metal washer, metal lid, steel wool, paper clip)

Directions for the activity:

Students will test the given items to determine whether they are conductors or insulators. They should look for similarities in the items that are insulators. Have them make predictions before testing the items. To set up the circuit, they can tape the stripped end of the wire to the bottom of the battery and tape the other end to the side of the metal base of the light bulb. Or use the recycled battery holder from a previous lesson.

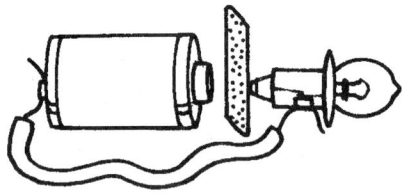

Responding to Discovery

Have students study their data. Discuss what the conductors have in common. Discuss what the insulators have in common. Can they make up a rule that would help identify which items are conductors and which are insulators? Discuss what this list has in common with the items that are magnetic.

Applications and Extensions

Think of ten additional items and predict whether they are conductors or insulators. Test each one.

Real-World Applications
Discuss how electrical wires are coated with plastic, which acts as an insulator.

Name _____

Conductors and Insulators

Big Question: Which items are conductors and which are insulators?

1. Tape the stripped end of the wire to the bottom of the battery. Tape the other end to the side of the metal base of the light bulb.

2. Predict whether each item is a conductor or an insulator.

3. Test each item by placing the item between the battery and the contact point of the light bulb. If the light bulb lights, the item you are testing is a conductor. An insulator will interrupt the circuit and the bulb will not light.

4. Record the results on the data table.

Item	Your prediction	Is it a conductor or an insulator?

🍂 What do all of the conductors have in common?

_____

🍂 What do all of the insulators have in common?

_____

🍂 What rule can you come up with to help identify items that are conductors and which are insulators?

_____

© Instructional Fair • TS Denison   IF20857 Electricity & Magnetism

Make Your Own Light bulb

Gearing Up
Pass some lamp bulbs around the classroom. Have the students study the filament and other inner workings. Pass around a burned-out bulb. Call students' attention to the broken filament. Compare that to the complete circuit they have been exploring in other lessons. Have students observe the glowing filament in a flashlight bulb that is lit.

> *Process Skills Used*
> - making a model
> - communicating
> - observing

Guided Discovery
Background for the teacher:
When electricity flows through the filament of an incandescent bulb, the filament gets hot. The heat energizes the atoms of the filament. These atoms give additional energy in the form of light. To identify the glowing filament up close, use a battery and a flashlight bulb.

Materials needed for each group:
a glass jar
modeling clay
two 30 cm wires with the ends stripped
10 cm nichrome wire (find in broken hair dryers or toasters or in a wire catalog from an electrical store)
two 3-inch (7.5-cm) nails
12-volt lantern battery

Directions for the activity:
Students follow the directions on page 31 to make a homemade light bulb. They are creating a complete circuit with the nichrome wire at the center. The nichrome wire provides the light. If the filament does not light in 15 seconds, have students check all the connections.

Responding to Discovery
Discuss how long it took for the filament to produce light. Discuss how you could make the light burn brighter. Compare the parts of the homemade bulb to a lamp bulb.

Applications and Extensions
Design a switch to turn the bulb on and off.

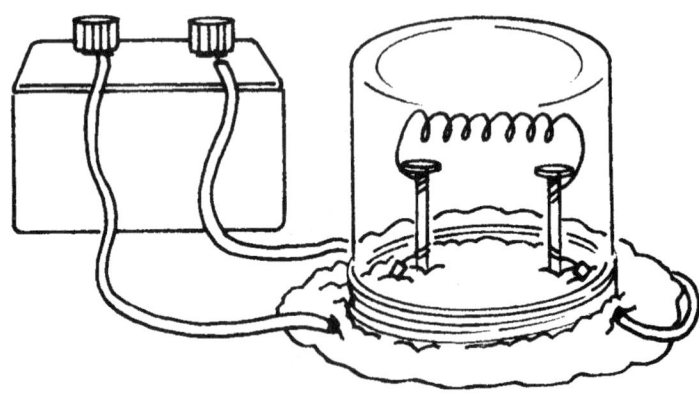

> *Real-World Applications*
> - Research Edison's original light bulb.
> - Show how most homes and buildings use a variety of forms of light, including incandescent, fluorescent, and neon.

© Instructional Fair • TS Denison

IF20857 *Electricity & Magnetism*

Name _____

Make Your Own Light Bulb

Big Question: What part of a bulb produces the light?

- Gather materials and make a homemade light bulb.

   1. Make a ball with the clay and flatten it so it is slightly larger than the mouth of the glass jar.

   2. Tightly wrap the nichrome wire around the nail so that the coils are not touching each other. Leave 2.5 cm of wire loose on each end to make the filament.

   3. Slide the filament wire off of the nail. Twist the loose ends around the heads of the nails.

   4. Stick the nails in the modeling clay. Secure one exposed end of each longer, insulated wire to the two nails.

   5. Place the jar over the nails and wires so that the free ends of longer wires trail outside the jar. Secure the jar in the modeling clay.

   6. Tape the other bare ends of the wires to the battery ends.

- Draw your light bulb.

- How long did it take for the filament to produce light? _____

- How could you make the light burn brighter? _____

- Which part of a light bulb produces the light? _____

- Explain how your setup works to produce light. _____

_____

© Instructional Fair • TS Denison   IF20857 *Electricity & Magnetism*

Static Electricity and Bubbles

Gearing Up

Ask the students to recall a time when they walked across a carpeted floor and received a shock by touching something? This is an example of static electricity. (Notice that if you touch the object again, you will not receive a second shock.) Ask two students to hold the four corners of a piece of plastic wrap. Have another student wipe the plastic with a tissue or wool cloth. Have the two students turn the plastic wrap over on top of a pile of small ripped pieces of paper. Observe what happens.

> *Process Skills Used*
> - drawing conclusions
> - recording data
> - collecting data
> - forming a hypothesis

Guided Discovery

Background for the teacher:

Static electricity occurs when an electric charge builds up on the surface of an object. When certain objects are rubbed together in a cool, dry environment, there is a transfer of electrons, or negative charges. In this discovery, the balloon picks up electrons and becomes negatively charged with static electricity.

Materials for each pair or group:

bubble solution and a wand (can be shared)

balloon

Directions for the activity:

Teacher tip: This might be a good outdoor activity.

One member of the group blows up the balloon and ties it closed. Have one student blow bubbles into the air toward the balloon. Students observe what happens. Next, one student should rub the balloon back and forth on his/her head five times. Then have a student blow bubbles into the air toward the balloon. Students observe what happens.

Responding to Discovery

Discuss what happened when the balloon was rubbed on the student's head. How did the bubbles act differently after the rubbing? Discuss how long the balloon held the charge that attracted the bubbles.

Applications and Extensions

Take a charged balloon and hold it against the wall. Let it go and see what happens.

> *Real-World Applications*
>
> Research how some people believe that static electricity may have been the cause of the explosion of the Hindenburg while it was docking in New Jersey.

© Instructional Fair • TS Denison

IF20857 *Electricity & Magnetism*

Name _____

Static Electricity and Bubbles

🍂 How do bubbles act around static electricity? _____

🍂 Blow up a balloon and tie it closed. Blow bubbles in the air and hold up the balloon. Draw what you observe.

🍂 Using the same balloon, rub it back and forth on the top of your head five times. Blow bubbles in the air again and hold the balloon nearby. Draw what you observe.

🍂 What do you think caused the bubbles to act like they did the second time?

_____

🍂 What happens when you rub the balloon again and hold it over some small bits of paper?

_____

🍂 What happens when you rub the balloon again and hold it against the wall?

_____

🍂 Touch the surface of the balloon with your hand and let go. Record what happens to the balloon on the wall.

_____

🍂 What happens when you rub the balloon on a different part of your body?

_____

🍂 Try rubbing the balloon more than five times. Record your observations.

_____

© Instructional Fair • TS Denison   IF20857 *Electricity & Magnetism*

Make Your Own Lightning

Gearing Up

Demonstrate static electricity. Comb your hair with a plastic comb. Hold the comb over a pile of small ripped paper pieces. Ask the students to observe and explain what happens.

Process Skills Used
- observing
- recording data
- simulating
- following directions
- calculating

Guided Discovery

Background for the teacher:

Lightning is a form of static electricity. In a storm cloud, moving air causes tiny water droplets and ice to rub together so they become charged with static electricity. The positive electrical charges float to the top of the cloud and the negative charges stay near the bottom of the cloud. This separation of electrical charges is very unstable. Lightning connects the negative charges in the cloud with the positive charges on the ground.

Materials for the demonstration:

A large iron or steel pot (not aluminum) with a plastic handle
rubber gloves
iron or steel fork
plastic sheet

Directions for the activity:

You will simulate lightning in this demonstration. Tape a plastic sheet to a tabletop. Put on rubber gloves and hold the pot by its insulated handle. Rub the pan vigorously back and forth on the plastic sheet. Do not touch the pan.

Holding the fork firmly in one hand and the pot in the other, bring the prongs slowly near the rim of the pot. When the gap between the pot and fork is small, a tiny spark should jump across. (Darken the room to see the spark more clearly.)

Responding to Discovery

Discuss the conditions that created the spark. Ask the students to think of how the pot and fork are like the cloud and the earth in a storm.

Applications and Extensions

Explain why lightning has a sound (thunder). Talk about thunderstorm safety. Calculate the distance of lightning in seconds and miles. A 5-second difference between the lightning flash and the thunder means the lightning struck 1 mile (1.6 km) away. For each additional 5 seconds, the strike is another mile away.

Real-World Applications
Discuss how you get carpet shocks.

Name _____

Make Your Own Lightning

- Draw what happened when the comb approached the paper pieces.

- Explain what happened when the fork nearly touched the pan.

  _____
  _____
  _____

- Draw a picture of the fork and pan.

- What are some ways that you can stay safe during a thunderstorm?

  _____
  _____
  _____
  _____
  _____
  _____

- How many miles away is the lightning if the thunder comes the following number of seconds behind the lightning?

  5 seconds =   ____ mile(s)

  10 seconds =   ____ mile(s)

  15 seconds =   ____ mile(s)

  20 seconds =   ____ mile(s)

  25 seconds =   ____ mile(s)

  30 seconds =   ____ mile(s)

© Instructional Fair • TS Denison   IF20857 *Electricity & Magnetism*

Performance-Based Assessment

3 = Exceeds expectations
2 = Consistently meets expectations
1 = Below expectations

Student Names

Lesson Investigation Discovery									
Lesson 1: Magnetic Attraction									
Lesson 2: Making a Compass									
Lesson 3: Mapping a Magnet									
Lesson 4: Magnetizing Metals									
Lesson 5: Magnetic Fields									
Lesson 6: Are All Metals Magnetic?									
Lesson 7: Is There Really Iron in Cereals?									
Lesson 8: Exploring Electromagnets									
Lesson 9: Recycled Battery Holder									
Lesson 10: Flashing the Light									
Lesson 11: Conductors and Insulators									
Lesson 12: Make Your Own Light Bulb									
Lesson 13: Static Electricity and Bubbles									
Lesson 14: Make Your Own Lightening									

Specific Lesson Skills									
Can make a reasonable hypothesis.									
Can identify the poles of a magnet.									
Can make detailed observations.									
Can propose an explanation.									
Can follow directions.									
Shows safe lab habits.									
Works well within a small group or class.									
Participates in discussions.									
Can record data gathered from investigations.									
Can classify data in meaningful categories.									
Can communicate through writing and/or drawing.									
Can apply what is learned to real-world situations.									

© Instructional Fair • TS Denison   IF20857 *Electricity & Magnetism*